To my first best friend who now lives in heaven. I carry you everywhere, especially in my heart. You taught me everything, except how to live without you.

How to use this book

The intended use of this book is for self-study, small groups, academic study, etc. No matter how you decide to use this book, you will find that you will grow to the extent that you are able to expand your mind, heart, and creativity. It is recommended that you take your time, discuss, think, challenge yourself, and others that you engage concerning this material. Take your insights into real world settings. Refuse to simply gain intellectual knowledge and understanding but employ practical application to your work in this book.

Suggested rules to follow:
- Pray before you start each lesson.
- Expect God to meet you, teach you, and grow you.
- Be open to the guidance of the Holy Spirit.
- Obey the promptings of the Holy Spirit as you read, study, and are convicted by the Word of God.
- Pray with an open mind and heart.
- Be honest with yourself, others, and God.
- Be open in your mind, heart, and spirit.
- Observe: your thoughts, emotions, physical sensations, urges, and judgements as you read and listen.
- Examine how you observe your own race, ethnicity, culture and how you fit into the text.
- Make attempts to observe yourself from other's perspective, culture, ethnicity, and context.

- Ask questions. Try to gain perspective.
- Be aware that you or no single person own the entire truth concerning race, racism, or healing.
- Share your experiences.
- Learn from others.
- Validate your own experiences.
- Validate other people's experiences.
- Understand that it is not necessary to agree. Simply understand an alternative perspective.
- Avoid judging (i.e., yourself, others, etc.)
- Accept yourself and your journey even if it looks different than others.
- Trust that God will guide you to where you need to be.
- Allow love to guide you in your interactions.

Note: Be open to writing your own or additional guidelines for using this book in your specific setting. You may find that you need more time on some lessons than others. If you are facilitating a small group, listen to your participants and their needs. Allow this to guide your use of the book much more than completing the lessons. The goal is application, not simply information.

Preface:

It has been an honor to write this devotional. It was such an emotional and spiritually liberating experience. There were several moments when I was writing about the historical events and had a visceral reaction to the horrific violence that so many Black people have endured. Many times, for no reason at all other than to attempt to live and prosper in life.

There were moments when I could relate on a deep unexplainable level with the pain in historical context, but also in the present. It is heart-breaking. I got the familiar feeling that so many of these historical events are being recreated with a new historical and cultural context. This is unnerving.

There were moments when I had to physically stop writing due to nausea, feeling so sick to my stomach at the hate, violence, and deplorable acts that were inflicted upon Black people. I felt in a sense that I was reliving each event as I wrote. There were moments when I just did not want to finish. It was too painful to have to see my people die such horrible deaths. I could see it. I could feel it. There is a part of them that is now living in me. I knew that no matter how much emotional pain that I had to endure, I must complete this book. I knew that I must preserve their stories, because hate was trying so diligently to erase them.

I thought to myself, "No brother I won't let them forget." I felt in my gut, "No sister, they must look history in the face and see." The stories that are shared in this book were selected because they, like many others, tell the story of the heinous terror that Blacks in America have and continue to endure when their only crime was given to them before they entered their mother's womb. Being Black...in America!

Many people forget the impact that trauma has upon the body, mind, and soul. We have lived generational trauma as a collective group. We are due for collective healing. The wounds that we suffer sometimes are hidden in the depths of our history and in the pain behind those beautiful dark eyes.

My hope and prayer for those reading this book is that God will meet you in powerful ways to bring truth and healing to your soul. May God grant you the grace to continue this journey beyond this book. May you have the courage to take the principles and your self-exploration into your daily living and relationships. May you be a true catalyst for change.

POEM

I see you.

For the little girl that has been broken and bruised, battered, and misused. I see you.

I see the pain in the hope hanging on by a thread in your eyes.

I see the fear that has suppressed the joy in your smile.

I see a world that looks at you and sees nothing while you hold on to despair because it's the only thing that you have left.

I see you.

You live in a world that wants to make you invisible and take away your voice, silencing you.

You have been taught to be seen and not heard. Yet you feel invisible.

You question whether people can actually see you, because you are background noise.

You sit with a broken dignity and crooked poise.

You fight daily for your own significance.

I see you.

As you act out in school and at home because that's the only way you know how to ask for help.

I see you.

Though they may label you a problem child they don't know the story of your survival.

They don't know that the people that were supposed to take care of you are your daily rivals.

They don't know that you had to be a parent while yet you were a kid. They are quick to call you grown and tell everyone what you did.

But no one has asked the question why is she...
Silent
Reserved
Untrusting
Feel unworthy
Anxious
Depressed
Suicidal
Irritated
And stressed?

Because she holds the weight of the world in her somatic complaint. Her stress lies in her stomachache...back ache...and headache...

Carry that pain in one hand and heavy expectations in the other. Juggle your self-respect and esteem. No one cares to ask what you think or what all of this means.

But...

I see you.
I hear you.

I will respond to you.
I will hold space for you.
I will be present for you.
I will not judge you.

Because...

You are worth it...regardless of what people say.
Regardless. Of. What. People. Say.
You are worth it!

I see you!

Day 1:
Calamity All Around, but Jesus on the Throne

Romans 12:12
"Rejoice in hope, be patient in
tribulation, be constant in prayer."

Every day that we turn on the news, we see calamity, racial injustice, devastation, mass shootings, and political corruption. The news that we receive is rarely good news. It is easy to get bogged down by the headlines and social media updates that seem to bring stress.

There are algorithms created by what we consume the most. Each click leads to more clicks of the same. It is challenging to have hope in a world like this. It is difficult to rejoice when all that we focus our eyes on is hopeless.

The Bible teaches us to be patient in tribulation. This is countercultural. There is so much suffering in the world. Patience is the last response expected. God requires more of us as believers.

There are people that will say that racism and social injustice do not exist. Another group says that racism will never end. Our Bible teaches us to rejoice in hope no matter what the world predicts.

We are still to be patient not only with the times, but with ourselves and one another. We are called to demonstrate love and patience to those that we agree with and disagree with alike.

In all of the uncertainty in the world, when believers have hope and patience, it brings hope to an otherwise hopeless world.

No matter the state of society, God is unchanging and sovereign. He has the power to manifest His word. But we must stay in constant communion with Him through prayer.

Prayer is our direct line to the throne of God. We have access to the Creator of the Universe and all of His divine nature. Certainly, our struggles and hangups are within His control.

Process Question:
When you have felt stressed and hopeless, have you prayed to God and asked for guidance?

Prayer for hope and patience:
Father, grant me the serenity to have patience and hope in times of hopelessness and tribulation. Help me to see your divine and sovereign power at work around me.

WRITE YOUR OWN PRAYER

WHAT THINGS BOTHER YOU
REGARDING THE STATE OF OUR
WORLD? BE SPECIFIC.

Day 2:
I Don't See Color

> ### John 12:40
>
> "He has blinded their eyes and made their hearts hard. Then they would not see with their eyes. They would not understand with their heart. They would not turn to Me. I could not heal them."

A common phrase that people have said is "I don't see color." It has been seen as a badge of anti-racism. However, in order to love your neighbors properly, it is important to be able to SEE them as God sees them. When we don't or refuse to see others the way that God intentionally and on purpose have fashioned them, we render them invisible to ourselves.

What happens when an entire race of people refuses to see or open their eyes to their blindness to racism and injustice? Not only do we miss an opportunity to love our neighbors and fulfill our divine purpose on this earth, but we also become complicit in their invisibility in society.

When people are invisible, they are present, but go unnoticed. They are present, but no one can see their needs, their hurts, their pain, and their struggles. Their attempts to reach out for help and support also go unnoticed. When an entire race of people become invisible, it is inevitable to trample upon them, not recognize, and continue. Why? Because they are invisible to you. It is not because they are not there. You just can't see THEM. You are blind to their gifts, talents, abilities, and all the things that God put there.

You may say, if I can't see the need then how can I meet it or how can I be held responsible? The truth is racism is one of the oldest sins in America. It is a generational sin that continues to be passed down. It inflicts generational trauma upon those that cannot be seen and that are rendered invisible.

Process Questions:

When people say that racism exists, what has been your response? Have you been the person that says, "I don't see color?" Or divert the conversation away from the sin of racism to spirituality? If so, you are complicit.

Consider day 2:

What things do you need to repent for?

Prayer of repentance:
Father, open my eyes to racism and the pain of
those affected by it. Open my eyes to ways that I
can help others to be seen and heard in my
areas of influence. Forgive me for being blind
and complicit in your children's pain.

Day 3:
Jesus Is Not an American

> **Romans 12:3**
>
> "For by the grace [of God] given to me I say to every one of you not to think more highly of himself [and of his importance and ability] than he ought to think; but to think so as to have sound judgment, as God has apportioned to each a degree of faith [and a purpose designed for service]."

Historically, America was favored and viewed with admiration. People have said that they aspire to have "the American Dream." People parade their American flags on their vehicles, homes, and businesses. In the National Anthem, we sing with pride "home of the free and land of the brave." What does this mean? How should we use the freedom that has been given to us?

While some view Americans as blessed people, there are others that view Americans as arrogant, rude, and materialistic. Hopefully, no Christian person would ever want to be viewed this way. While traveling back from a mission trip, I witnessed a missionary in an international airport push past a long line of people, disregard the airline's requests to stop, and proclaim loudly to other missionaries "We don't have to wait in line. We are Americans. Use your privilege." What a stunning and appalling thing to think, much less say. What a poor representation of Jesus and disregard for people.

I thought to myself. What if Jesus was in this line? Jesus was not an American. Does this mean because we are Americans, we have the right to trample over other human beings? The answer of course is "absolutely not!" It is dangerous to think more highly of ourselves than we ought to when it comes to race, ethnicity and cultural differences.

Arrogance is blinding. It makes people tone deaf to opportunities to exercise the fruit of the spirit. Being loving to others requires sound judgment. To have power and to choose to be loving and gentle over misusing and abusing it for selfish gain is a true virtue.

Looking down upon or disregarding another human being takes little spiritual effort. It takes no self-discipline. Love is not required to push past others to avoid your own discomfort. It carries with it an attitude of "I am better than you." This is superiority. By default, if someone is superior then there must be an inferior (person). God is not pleased with the type of behavior that places a high degree of respect for self and diminishes the value of others. It demonstrates low cultural and spiritual intelligence.

Prayer for humility:
Father, help me to use the grace that you
have given me to be humble and loving
towards others no matter their station in life.
Help me to never think of myself more
highly than another person. Help me to see
the value that you see in each individual and
demonstrate love on every occasion.

Consider day 3:

Concerning your lifestyle, what things have you
judged superior to others of different races? Be
specific.

Day 4:
The Most Segregated Hour

Galatians 3:28

"There is [now no distinction in regard to salvation] neither Jew nor Greek, there is neither slave nor free, there is neither male nor female; for you [who believe] are all one in Christ Jesus [no one can claim a spiritual superiority]."

It is said that the most segregated hour is during the Sunday church service. People gather from all over the world to attend church services and worship God. Yet, while we all are Christians and worship the same God, one must question, why must we be so segregated?

Many races, ethnicities, and cultures intermingle during the week in the marketplace or at least in a parallel fashion in proximity; however, on the day that we worship our Lord and Savior, we are separated and divided. This is not the heart of Jesus. Jesus died for all who love and accept Him. If it has been made clear that there is no separation of God's people, why do we work so hard to remain separate?

Salvation is the most important gift of our faith. Jesus desires that every person, no matter their race, ethnicity, socioeconomic status, or gender, that everyone come into a relationship with Him as Lord and Savior. While intellectually, we may know and even believe this, in practice our biases, prejudice, and racism prevent us from shining our best light in the world. It is entirely possible to have the same denomination in the same area, but they never intermingle because of demographic differences. How sad is this?

Process Questions:

How often have you hindered the mission of the Church by being stuck in your comfort zone?

.

Are you more comfortable staying with people that look like, talk like, and act like you?

How often do you step outside of your comfort zone and engage other believers that do not fit your demographic?

Prayer for equality:

Father, help me to see the differences in people as a divine gift from you. Help me to see and value people the way that you value them. Help me not to develop a superior attitude of myself over your children. Guide me in seeing the soul of your children rather than race, ethnicity, gender, and socioeconomic status first.

Consider day 4:

Concerning your life, what things have you considered spiritually superior to others of different races, cultures, and ethnic groups? Be specific.

Day 5:
One Race

One of the most famous stories in the Bible is the creation story of Adam and Eve. It is a beloved story in children's ministries all over the world. In the innocence of children, many have asked, how did we get so many races if all people came from Adam and Eve? This is a great and enlightening question.

The Bible is clear that every nation of people came to earth through one man and one woman. So where did race come from? Race in its basic sense is a social construct. This means that it was created, man-made. It was based on theory and prejudice as a means of separating and degrading some while uplifting and prizing others.

Why would one construct something that has caused so much division, death, and conflict in the world?

In a natural sense, the answer to this question is capital gain.

As scripture says, "for the love of money is the root of all kinds of evil." In a physical sense, to create caste systems of hierarchy to gain and maintain social power. In a spiritual sense, it is the greatest socialized sin. The motive of Satan is to kill, steal, and destroy. He has successfully used race and racism to accomplish his purpose in the earth.

Process Questions:

How often have you assisted Satan in his purpose?

How do you view racism?

Do you think that it is a sin?

Are you guilty of the sin of racism?

God designed His creation beautifully and said, "it is very good." There have been race wars, riots, brutalization, and disasters as a result of racial division and conflict. So, how can something that was intended to be beautiful cause so much destruction? In short, Satan loves to take what God has meant for good and use it for evil.

Prayer for unity:

Father, help me to be mindful of all of your creation. Help me to see others that look different than me as my brothers and sisters, my divine family. Help me not to set barriers in my life to segregate me from your children. Help us to remove boundaries that you did not set.

Consider day 5:

In what ways have you separated yourself from people of differing racial and ethnic backgrounds? Be specific.

Day 6:
My God is My Judgement

In a day and age where technology is revered, it is easy to get on any device to comment on the photos and lives of others without a second thought of the impact of our judgements. We have simplified communication to the point of using emojis to give our opinions. We can even create alternate accounts to give our honest, unfiltered commentary, many times saying things online that would never be said in person.

When we judge, it exposes our own weaknesses. It puts our heart on display. When we judge others based on their race and ethnic features, the Bible says that this is superficial and arrogant. It warns against this.

When we are angry, it is easier to use judgmental and harsh language. It is especially easy to do this when we disagree or hold differing views. God's word is unchanging. If it was wrong then, it is wrong now. Judging others based on appearance is a sin. Moreover, judging and discriminating against others is also a violation of the Love commandment.

It has been said that people get additional courage to be rude and say what they really think when they are in the comfort of their homes hiding behind their devices. This is both arrogant and foolish. While those online may not be able to see the person behind the comments, God sees everything. God sees the hidden motives that people have in the heart. He knows the thoughts that we have.

When we judge we are not acting in love for our neighbors. When we judge others, we are violating the law of love for ourselves also.

Our judgments have a way of not only poisoning those that hear them, but they also poison us. It is true, "death and life are in the power of the tongue." Judgements have a way of killing, particularly if they are unkind or mean-spirited.

Racial slurs are judgements based on appearance or traits with the intent to degrade others. God is not pleased with this. If God calls His creation "good", who are we to say otherwise?

Process Questions:

How often do you resist the urge to hold back your judgments of others?

How do you judge others when you are angry?

Would God be pleased with the judgements that flow from your heart?

Take a moment to journal about the impact that judgments from others have had upon you.

Consider day 6:

Concerning other races, what judgement have you had. Be specific.

Day 7:
Love A Commandment And Not a Suggestion

Romans 2:11

"For God shows no partiality [no arbitrary favoritism; with Him one person is not more important than another]."

As a child, you likely had a best friend or a favorite toy that you spent your time and attention on. Like children, what we love will get our time and attention. In another sense "where your treasure is, that is where your heart will be also." It is difficult for us to separate our hearts from the things that we love.

God is Love. It is not something that He does. It is who He is. As the Creator of the Universe, God makes it clear throughout scripture that He loves us. He said that when he finished creating, that "it is good." With the creation of Adam and Eve, he referred to His creation as "very good." He demonstrated value in humans by giving his image to us. We are all image-bearers of God. This means that we are to be His representatives in the earth.

God is not like people. People have favorites. But this is not like God. He shows no favoritism. He does not value anyone more than another. Certainly, because God created all of us, He would not show more value in one race over another or one ethnicity above another. God holds none to be more superior than another. So why do we?

This is like trying to say that the part of God that is in me is better and superior to the part of God that is in you. This makes no sense. We are all image-bearers of God. Since God is Love, He cannot love some of His creations more than others. It goes against His very nature. Certainly, He does not want us doing this either. This cannot be true agape love. Instead, this is love based on conditions. It says, if you meet my conditions, then I will love you. This is not love. People recognize us by the way that we love.

Process Questions:

What conditions have you placed on your love?

Do you love based on how another person looks?

Have you decided how much you love based on a person's background?

How do you love others of different racial and ethnic backgrounds than yours?

Would God be pleased with the judgements that flow from your heart?

Take a moment to journal your response to the above question.

Love is a commandment, not a suggestion. We are commanded to Love God with our whole heart, soul, mind, and strength. And to love our neighbors as we love ourselves. In God's economy Loving Him means obedience to what He says. We hold no race or people to be more superior than another. We are called to love. Refusing to love or withholding love by showing partiality is a sin.

Consider day 7:

What ways have you demonstrated conditional self love? Be specific.

Prayer for equality:
Father, I ask for forgiveness for showing favorites in how I love. Give me the heart to love purely like you love no matter the race or ethnic background. Help me to be a true image-bearer and representative for your Kingdom everywhere that I go.

Day 8:
Particularly Privileged

Acts 10:34-35

"Opening his mouth, Peter said:

"Most certainly I understand now that God is not one to show partiality [to people as though Gentiles were excluded from God's blessing], 35 but in every nation the person who fears God and does what is right [by seeking Him] is acceptable and welcomed by Him."

Has someone that you know ever had a party or event and you were not invited? It would be easy to feel excluded as partygoers share their memories and pictures of the event while you passively watch and listen. This is such a lonely feeling. To have others be apart while you are on the outside of the discussion. The pain of exclusion can be so hard to deal with. Imagine that this was not an isolated incident, but rather a way of life. No matter where you go or what you do, you are never quite on the inside. That can be an isolating and disconnected life.

Many people of marginalized communities understand exactly what this feels like when they leave their homes and go into the marketplace. While the majority may feel included, the people that are not are often unnoticed. It is difficult to feel left out, but to go unnoticed in the process, the pain of loneliness can feel even more intense.

White privilege, for some, is a blessing. But while those that are blessed by it are reaping the benefits, there are those that are not so blessed and do not get the benefits. In fact, they are isolated from what white privilege may afford others without additional work or effort. In these cases, it would be easy for those with privilege to enjoy their benefits while others go unnoticed. This too can also be very isolating. There is a difference between those enjoying the benefits of privilege and those suffering from the pain of disadvantage. While privilege is not earned and may not be intentional, it has an impact on those that do not share in the same benefits but occupy the same space.

White privilege is such a large topic of discussion that many people do not know what to do once they realize that they have it. Like the people who attended the party, it simply takes mindfulness of looking around and recognizing who is impacted by the privilege and making a conscious decision to do the right thing and include those that do not share it. This is an act of love, demonstrating God's character intentionally.

God does not show partiality. He includes rather than excludes.

Process Questions:

What areas of privilege do you have?

How does your privilege impact others who do not share in the privilege?

Have you been willing to use your privilege to help or benefit those that do not have privilege as an act of love?

Consider day 8:

What ways can you use the privileges that you have to love others? Be specific.

Prayer of love:
Father, help me to avoid excluding people. Help me to see my areas of privilege and use it to benefit others who do not have it. Give me insight on how I can love others more by including them and helping them to avoid feeling isolated and lonely while in my presence.

Write your own prayer concerning privilege:

Day 9:

Subhuman and Superior

> **John 13:34**
>
> **"I am giving you a new commandment, that you [a]love one another. Just as I have loved you, so you too are to love one another."**

Currently, we use the word "love" to describe how we feel about any and everything. It is not uncommon to hear people say that they love everything from going to the beach to a brand of clothing. When a word is overused and used in multiple contexts, it can lose the true essence and be lost in translation.

A common misconception is that love is a feeling. It is used in the context of demonstrating a relationship to a person and what they say that they love. Love in fact, biblically is an action word. When we are commanded to love, it does not mean that God is telling us to feel a certain way about a person. It means that we are to behave in a way that demonstrates His character towards them.

One may ask, who is God talking about when He says "one another?" This means everyone. No one is excluded in God's commandment. For we are all His creation and God is impartial. He has no favorites. He wants us to demonstrate His love the way that He would to His creation.

Throughout history eugenicists attempted to increase the likelihood of improving the human race by joining favored characteristics, which were racially biased towards people of color and emphasized Caucasian traits. It expanded the notion that White people were the superior race. It birthed the idea that the Black race was not human.

Using dehumanization throughout history has been a cornerstone of racism. This idea has been employed as a means of enslaving, raping, beating, and brutalizing Africans brought to America during the Transatlantic Slave Trade. This was not a demonstration of love. If anything, it is the direct opposite. And it was widely accepted and practiced, oftentimes also by Christians.

American history is not always the most palatable. Even then, the Word of God was still true. Christians were expected to love others. Enslaved Africans were included in "others." Why was this not challenged more in the Christian church? Even more prevalent, why were Christians engaging in such unimaginable and deplorable acts? In short, cognitive dissonance. This is a term that basically means that in order to accept something that goes against what a person believes, they must change the narrative to make it more acceptable so they can continue doing the behavior. For instance, it is possible for a Christian to enslave, beat and murder an enslaved African if they convince themselves that Africans are subhuman and property. The thought was they can do whatever they want with their property.

This is why it is vital that we understand the meaning of God's view of love as people "love" everything under the sun and this is more of a feeling than a conscious decision of moral behavior towards our fellow man...God's children.

Process Questions:

What areas of cognitive dissonance have you had that has kept you from loving other races the way that God has commanded you to love?

How does viewing "love" as a commandment impact your decision to treat others with the same respect that you want?

What do you think the world would look like if the world loved the way that Jesus loves?

Prayer for obedience:
Father, help me to love the way that you have commanded me to love other races. Help me to understand the true meaning of love and how to do it purposely every day. Help me to see people and their humanity and not take away from them what you have freely given, freedom. Help me to love in a way that helps to heal their pain.

Day 10:

Distinctively Diverse

> **Romans 10:12**
>
> "For there is no distinction between Jew and Gentile; for the same Lord is Lord over all [of us], and [He is] abounding in riches (blessings) for all who call on Him [in faith and prayer]."

Have you ever witnessed a parent playing favorites with their children? It can be a difficult thing to watch as it would likely have a damaging effect on the children and their relationship. Just as no good parent would intentionally make a distinction in their children through favorable treatment, God does not do this either. What God does for one of His children, He will do for another.

God desires all of His children to be blessed and carry His favor. Not just some and leaving others out. Likewise, we are not to treat God as if He belongs solely to us and exclude others based on our human standards. God does not take kindly to people mistreating His children. That includes his other children.

If you have ever put two children in a room for a period, it would not be long before there is a conflict of some sort. A good parent does not want to see their children arguing, fighting, and living in strife. It would break the heart of the parent. When we are having difficulty getting along with our brothers and sisters in Christ, it does break the heart of God. He is our heavenly father. He wants to see all His children prosper and do well. God loves to see His children loving and supporting one another.

When God sees us fighting and carrying on as if He is not our father, this displeases Him. Even more so, when we are using our differences to make distinctions towards ourselves and one another, this displeases God. God created everyone in His image. It breaks the heart of God when His children use the gifts that He gave them to create beauty and diversity for evil, it is dishonoring to Him. We are only criticizing and abusing our heavenly father's creation.

Ezekiel 18:20
"The person who sins [is the one that] will die. The son will not bear the punishment for the sin of the father, nor will the father bear the punishment for the sin of the son; the righteousness of the righteous shall be on himself, and the wickedness of the wicked shall be on himself."

There is no need for Christians to distinguish ourselves from others who are of a different race than we are to gain anything whether that is a job, title, housing, etc. God is rich in blessings, and He will not withhold anything good from those that love him. He has enough for everyone of His children. There is no need to compare ourselves or compete. God loves all of us and wants to see us all thriving and loving Him as well as each other.

Consider day 10:

What ways have you compared yourself or competed with people of other races? Be specific.

Prayer for acceptance:
Father, help me to see beauty in diversity. Help me to see your image in all other races and accept them as my Kingdom family. Instead of distinguishing myself from others, help me to honor you by loving them and all that they bring to the table without comparing myself and feeling the need to compete. Help me to trust that you will take care of me and my needs.

Day 11:
Legally Corrupt

Ezekiel 18:20

"The person who sins [is the one that] will die. The son will not bear the punishment for the sin of the father, nor will the father bear the punishment for the sin of the son; the righteousness of the righteous shall be on himself, and the wickedness of the wicked shall be on himself."

It is no secret that enslaved Africans were subjected to 400 years of free servitude and legally deemed property of White slave owners in America. How is it that after 400 years of free labor Black Americans have been labeled "lazy"? Even post slavery, Black Americans were terrorized, jailed, and murdered by rogue White mobs. Many Blacks were considered criminals because of the color of their skin and being in places that Whites did not want them to be. In a lecture based on the book White Fragility, Robin DiAngelo makes the statement "We project our sin onto the Black body...lazy...criminal...murderer."

The law has the power to deem behavior legal; however, this is according to man. Most assuredly those in positions of power determine what is considered legal and illegal, while preserving the power and subservient state of Black people. Even though man may believe it is a good idea, it is not a good idea to God. Sin is sin. While man tries to justify and excuse away their behavior, God sees what is in your heart.

What we now know as the police was an institution made for the purpose of catching slaves. They were known as slave patrols. In this time, the word "criminal" would have been used to identify those that sought their freedom "unlawfully". "Criminal" would not have been a term used towards the slavers that stole human beings from their homes, sold, brutalized, murdered, raped, and beat enslaved Black people. While slavery was legal, it was still sin.

Each person must be accountable for their own sin. Many people may be tempted to say that since they were not slave owners, they have no part in racism. This may be true; however, do you consider the impact of your behavior upon others?

Process Questions:

How often do you participate in systems that uphold racist laws, ideas, and systemic structures of oppression?

Have you been okay with the oppression of others as long as you benefit from it?

Consider day 11:

What structures of oppression have you supported?
Be specific.

Prayer of repentance:
Father, help me to recognize the
role that I play in upholding the sin
of racism. Allow your Word to be a
mirror unto me, shining light in the
areas where I have been blind and
chosen to not see. Forgive me for
allowing my sin to harm others and
corrupt my own soul.

Write a prayer of repentance for supporting the
systemic oppression of God's children.

Day 12:
Constitutional Corruption

Genesis 1:26-27

"26 Then God said, "Let Us (Father, Son, Holy Spirit) make man in Our image, according to Our likeness [not physical, but a spiritual personality and moral likeness]; and let them have complete authority over the fish of the sea, the birds of the air, the cattle, and over the entire earth, and over everything that creeps and crawls on the earth." 27 So God created man in His own image, in the image and likeness of God He created him; male and female He created them."

Article one, section two of the United States Constitution deemed enslaved Black people three-fifths of a person. This was instituted as a means of allowing White slave owners the ability to use their slaves to count towards political power in determining representation in government. The Three-fifths Compromise was an attempt to hold political power, economic gain, and place value on Black bodies.

All people were created in the image of God after His spiritual and moral likeness. How is it that in a nation where it prints on its money, "In God We Trust"; however, enslave Black people and deemed them less than a human being? How is it that human beings were allowed to be sold for the same currency that claims to put its trust in God? Does God place a higher value on some races over others? Over some human beings? Absolutely not! Nowhere in scripture can you find this to be the case.

Certainly, when God gave man dominion in the earth, He did not mean for this dominion to be over other human beings. God never intended for human beings to control or have power over other humans. This is a part of the fall of man. Man's attempt to act as gods in the earth and Lord over others. It is idolatry. White supremacy and superiority are forms of idolatry. White slavers forced their slaves to call them Master. The word "master" can be synonymous with "Lord".

White supremacy is the belief that the White race is the superior race and should dominate other human beings and society. Racism and racist ideas can be systemic through voting practices, structures, and systems that ensure that White supremacy is upheld to maintain a permanent position of social and political power. Another way of saying this is dominion in the earth. This is not God-ordained dominion, but man-made, which is sin.

When considering systems of power, how do you benefit from them?

How have you used positions of power to gain control over others?

Consider day 12:

What racist ideas have you or your family held? Be specific.

Prayer of Repentance:
Father, thank you for giving me dominion in the earth. Help me to keep a pure attitude and humble heart concerning your people. Give me the humility to not place myself over another person in thought, speech, or deed. Help me to honor my divine nature and the divine nature of others.

Write a prayer of repentance for supporting racist policies and ideas.

Day 13:
Perfectly Prejudice

James 2:1

"My fellow believers, do not practice your faith in our glorious Lord Jesus Christ with an attitude of partiality [toward people—show no favoritism, no prejudice, no snobbery]."

Research shows that racial prejudice and discrimination impact the brain and body in harmful ways. Many people of color who experience racial discrimination and prejudice are often invalidated and questioned regarding their experiences. This may add an additional layer of mental and emotional distress. Racial prejudice and injustice are highly linked to anxiety and depression.

Research indicates that the body and brain is not made for consistent and persistent stress, which is often the experience of people of color in America related to racial prejudice. People who have been the target of violence, intimidations, and social oppression also exhibit traumatic stress and more physical health issues like hypertension, heart problems, and Gastrointestinal issues.

The Bible is clear in discussing the position that race and discrimination has. It warns us to avoid discriminating against one another. This violates the law of love, which is the most important commandment next to loving God.

1 John 4:8 says, "Anyone who does not love does not know God, because God is love."

This may sound harsh; however, the way that we love or fail to love one another is a direct indication of our spiritual maturity or immaturity. Many people can "love" with their words; however, God looks not only at the words, but actions and the heart motives.

Process Questions:

How often have you secretly judged a person based on their appearance?

Have you looked at their cultural or racial distinctions and pre-judged them?

These are not acts of love, but of judgment. God is our judge, not people. When we put ourselves in the position of judging another, we are giving ourselves the job of being God. This is pride!

Prayer for humility:
Father, help me to glorify you in my thoughts, speech, and behaviors towards others that are different from me. Help me not place judgment. Reveal my prejudice to me so that I will not be the cause of harm to my brothers and sisters in Christ.

Identify 7 ways that you can practice more humility concerning racial diversity and inclusion of others.

How have you seen racism
impact trauma in society?

What has been the impact upon
you? Be specific.

Day 14:
Counterfeit Christian

1 Corinthians 13:1

"If I speak with the tongues of men and of angels but have not [a]love [for others growing out of God's love for me], then I have become only a noisy gong or a clanging cymbal [just an annoying distraction]."

Many people can attest to seeing a person that is constantly talking about God, but it is only talk. There is nothing more embarrassing to Bible believing Christians than to have a person claim Christianity but act like the devil in their treatment of people. More than anything this confuses non-believers and gives Christianity a bad name.

When people listen to and make racist jokes or comments in your presence how often have you laughed or participated? If you bear the name of Christ and have taken part in this type of behavior, you are a hypocrite. This gives a false impression of who Jesus is and who Christians are.

The KKK started as a Christian group. They preached white supremacy and anti-black hate. While they professed Christianity, their speech and actions were far from godly behavior. To an unbeliever this is confusing. How can a person preach about the love of God and use their mouth and bodies to bring about hate? To the world this is confusing and annoying. It provides little hope in the God that we serve. We are essentially driving people away from Christ.

We are called to be image bearers of Christ in this world. When we misrepresent Christ, we do more harm to the kingdom of God than an "evil person" that does not bear the name of Christ. Believe it or not people watch our behavior and make determination of whether they want to follow the God that we say we serve.

Process Questions:

Are you turning people on to God or causing them to repel him?

How has your behavior impacted others around you?

Have you been a good representation of who God is?

Prayer for truth:
Father, help me to display your love
in truth and to represent you in a way
that is honorable. Help me to lead
others to Jesus by the way that I lead
my life publicly and privately.

List comments that you have said or thought
that have not been a good representation of
God.

What areas do you need to repent for concerning displaying racist ideas (i.e. joking, voting, comments, policies, etc.)

Day 15:
Blessed to Be a Blessing

1 Corinthians 13:2

"And if I have the gift of prophecy [and speak a new message from God to the people], and understand all mysteries, and [possess] all knowledge; and if I have all [sufficient] faith so that I can remove mountains, but do not have love [reaching out to others], I am nothing."

In today's culture it is easy to be impressed with the many gifts and talents that people possess. We can watch the lives of others from across the world through social media and video conferences. While all of these things are not inherently bad, we can sometimes get off focus. We can place a higher value on one person's gift while devaluing another. And this was never God's intent.

The purpose of any gift that has been God-given is to glorify Him and uplift his people. When we use what God has given us to look down upon others or to get vainglory for ourselves, we miss the mark. It doesn't matter how much we know or can do, if we do not love others like Christ loves His church, we have failed in our mission.

When we fail to reach out to others and share the gifts that we have been given based on who we believe is worthy or who has favor with us, we are using discrimination. Whether this discrimination is racial, ethnic, or based on physical characteristics that are different from our own, it is a sin.

Anything that God gives us is to be used for His glory and His purposes. When we abuse the gifts that we have been given, this displeases God. It is particularly heinous when we have used God's gifts to discriminate against His children or to make them feel less than.

We are called to reach out to others. This is the evidence of the love that we have as Christians. When we fail to reach out to others and instead reach in, we are missing opportunities to display the love of Christ in the world and build bridges to people that are not like us.

Process Questions:

How often have you taken an opportunity to reach out to a brother or sister in Christ that is not a part of your congregation?

How often have you reached out to the brothers and sisters in Christ that are of a different socioeconomic class, racial background, or cultural ethnicity than yours?

To God, we are all His children. He is glorified when we come together. At these moments He is in our mist and healing takes place.

Prayer for connection:
Father, help me to use the gifts and abilities that you have given me to be a blessing to brothers and sisters in Christ that look nothing like me. Soften my heart and help me to invite them in rather than exclude them.

List 5 people that you can intentionally connect with to build a bridge of racial and ethnic inclusion.

Day 16:
Perverted Justice

Leviticus 19:15 MSG

"Don't pervert justice. Don't show favoritism to either the poor or the great. Judge on the basis of what is right."

In the state of Ohio, April 1, 1807, Black Laws were instituted to prevent Black people from testifying in court against a White person. These laws were paramount in restricting not only Black movement, but also Black wealth. It made Black people vulnerable to White abuse and terror with impunity. Basically, it became legal for White people to bring frivolous lawsuits, harass, and brutalize Black people without fear of punishment from the law. The law failed to prosecute White on Black crimes and kept Black people who were eyewitnesses from testifying.

Justice is based on the law. But what happens when the law is discriminatory in nature? What type of justice can a person get from a system that was never meant to help or serve them or what is considered right, just, and fair? This is what is considered a perverted justice system. The word perverted means to "lead astray morally." Many people believe that if it is legal, then it must be right; however, this is not always true.

Morality cannot be legislated. There must be a higher law than the one that is man-made, which is built upon finite knowledge and human prejudice. God's law is higher than man's law. God's law seeks to bring true justice that is not based on favoritism, discrimination, or fixed outcomes. God's justice is based on what is considered right according to His standards, preserving Holiness and righteousness.

Unfortunately, today many people are not interested in God's standards of righteousness and justice. There is a growing disdain for what God desires and sees as right and wrong. The word "justice" has been perverted to such a degree that it can be sold to the highest bidder or given to those that have a higher social status. While many people would agree that this is not fair, it is a reality that people that are not financially endowed understand. Laws can be created to serve the best interest of those in power and disadvantage those with little or no power.

Process Questions:

When you have seen injustice have you spoken out about it?

What laws have you supported that have placed people at a disadvantage?

How would you feel if you could not depend on the law to protect you?

How does it impact you as a Christian to know that the legal system was designed to protect those in power and exploit the vulnerable?

Prayer for Courage:
Father, help me to not remain silent when I see injustice. Give me the courage to speak out against exploitation of the vulnerable. Help me to stand up for what is right and Holy in your sight.

List 5 ways that you can demonstrate courage
to fight against racism.

How will you specifically implement these
ideas?

Day 17:
Lady Injustice

Proverbs 20:10

"Differing weights [one for buying and another for selling] and differing measures, Both of them are detestable and offensive to the Lord."

If you have ever gone to any court in America, you have probably seen Lady Justice. She is typically seen blindfolded, which symbolizes justice being blind and free from bias and with balanced scales. While this is an idealistic image, we know that people are not blind and without bias. While justice may be blind, the people that sit on many juries and decide the fate of others, are not.

Nearly 2 million people have been imprisoned in the United States. This population is disproportionately Black. This is not necessarily due to an increase in crime committed by Black people, but rather misguided legislation and sentencing laws that impact Black people at a higher rate than Whites and other races. This has detrimental effects on other institutions in society for Black people: education, finances, family structure, housing, job prospects, etc.

When laws are created that put Black people at a disadvantage in nearly every front of society, this is a cause for concern. When laws are created to criminalize behavior or people, this has the impact of creating a culture that supports laws of the same. In other words, if you can criminalize a public health issue like substance abuse, then not only are people not receiving treatment, they are imprisoned for having an addiction.

The 1986 Anti-Drug Abuse Act was a law passed that gave harsher sentences for crack than the powder form of the same drug. The law was enacted based on the epidemic of crack use in the "urban" or Black and Brown communities. Powder cocaine was viewed as a drug abused by White people and people of a higher socioeconomic status. Sentencing for the possession of this drug was typically less time. While this may appear to be an attempt to decrease substance use, this law did not address addiction, but rather criminalized addiction. And resulted in mass incarceration of Black and Brown people.

God respects no one differently than another. This is injustice on many levels and is detestable in the sight of God.

How do you view addiction?

When you see a person with an addiction do you have a negative view of them?

How do you judge their addiction and them as people?

Are they seen as of lower value in your eyes? Why or why not?

Prayer for forgiveness:
Father, forgive me for allowing my view of people who are suffering to be corrupted. Forgive me for turning a blind eye to those that have been victimized by the legal system. Help me to have the courage to do what is right in your sight and not be a party to things that you view as detestable.

What ways do you think criminalizing substance abuse support racist ideas?

How do you believe that this impacts the expression of racism in society?

Day 18:
Divided We Stand

John 3:16

"For God so [greatly] loved and dearly prized the world, that He [even] gave His [One and] [a]only begotten Son, so that whoever believes and trusts in Him [as Savior] shall not perish, but have eternal life."

One of the many joys of coming of age and gaining independence for many people is buying a first home. It can be a wonderful experience. Everything from finding the right neighborhood, school system, parks, and attractions that meet the family's needs. What happens when your choices are limited or predetermined not by costs alone, but where the government says that you are allowed to live? It has the capacity to impact the quality of life and livelihood.

In the 1930s, the federal government instituted practices that used blatant discriminatory housing practices ensuring home loans to White Americans while denying loans to Black Americans. This process is called Redlining. The government-sponsored Homeowners' Loan Corporation and the

Federal Home Loan Bank Board used maps with redlines indicating neighborhoods to determine which neighborhoods were worthy of investments. Black neighborhoods were viewed as dangerous and less desirous for making investments.

The intent in this practice was to keep America segregated. This decreased the property value of Black and Brown neighborhoods and increased the value of White neighborhoods. More economic resources were funneled to the White neighborhoods while scarce resources were available in the Black and Brown neighborhoods.

It was never God's intent for His people to be segregated on the earth based on race. God does not show partiality in His children. He has no desire for people to do this to one another either. There will be no segregated neighborhoods in Heaven. Jesus died for all who believe in Him as Lord and Savior. This is the only qualifier for admittance into the Kingdom of Heaven.

Process Questions:

When you look around your neighborhood, how much diversity is there?

How much interaction do you have with people of diverse backgrounds?

How do you view diversity in your neighborhood? Job? Church? Family?

Prayer for unity:
Father, unite your children on earth as it is in heaven. Help us to not segregate ourselves from one another. Give us the grace to accept one another and embrace the differences that you created.

Day 19:
Racism Is Not My Problem

Matthew 7:12

"So then, in everything treat others the same way you want them to treat you, for this is [the essence of] the Law and the [writings of the] Prophets."but have eternal life."

Jane Elliot is an American Educator and famous for her Blue Eye Experiment. In one of her presentations, she asked "If you, as a White person, would like to be treated the way Black people are treated in this society, stand." The room was silent. No one moved. She repeated the question, to which no one stood. She then exclaimed that "White people are not ignorant to the treatment of Blacks in America." Her assertion was that they must have some awareness of the distinction between the way that Whites and Blacks are treated in America. Further, given this knowledge, they know that they would not want to trade places or be treated similarly.

The question becomes, how is it that people can be aware of the maltreatment of other human beings and passively watch the injustice? Jane Elliot makes the comment, "it is not a problem unless it affects you." How true is this for you? Are you bothered by what happens to others as long as it doesn't impact you?

In her Blue Eye Experiments, she attempts to demonstrate the impact of discrimination and preferential treatment of some and not others. Overwhelmingly, in experiment after experiment the results are the same, people given preferential treatment begin to adopt superior attitudes and treat the others as if they are inferior.

This is a small example of how racial prejudice and discrimination has functioned in society. Racism can be internalized whether a person is viewed as superior or inferior. This is displeasing to God! Any good parent, when they hear that their child is engaging in undesirable behavior, utters the words "treat people the way that you want to be treated." This is not much different from what is mentioned in Matthew 22:39, which commands us to "love our neighbors as we love ourselves."

If the maltreatment of one human being is not something that we would accept for ourselves, then what makes it acceptable for another person, no matter their race? This is not functioning in the law of Love.

Process Questions:

How often have you allowed others to be mistreated in your presence without a second thought or intervention?

What do you think motivates others to passively standby and allow maltreatment of others?

How do you view diversity in your neighborhood? Job? Church? Family?

How do you feel when you experience discrimination or unfair treatment?

What ways have you seen
African Americans treated unfairly in society?
Explain.

What do you think the role of a Christian is when others are treated unfairly in society? Explain.

Day 20:
Beauty Is In The Eye

2 Corinthians 10:12 NLT

"Oh, don't worry; we wouldn't dare say that we are as wonderful as these other men who tell you how important they are! But they are only comparing themselves with each other, using themselves as the standard of measurement. How ignorant!"

Black people in America have been the source of discrimination through European emphasized standards of beauty for centuries. It has targeted the shape of Black bodies, hair texture, and ethnic traits that are specific to Black people. Well, the saying goes "beauty is in the eye of the beholder," what happens when European standards of beauty are used to exclude Black people from making progress?

For many people of color, these imposed standards of ethnic and racial discrimination have detrimental effects on real life circumstances. There have been many cases of hair discrimination, which has resulted in Black people not getting jobs, winning tournaments, and being excluded from promotion in multiple fields.

This is not a new problem, racial discrimination through European imposed standards of beauty has been weaponized for centuries. The goal historically has been to inferiorize Black people. The way that a person looks, their hair, body type, and skin color are all things that are God-given. These are not things that can be changed with ease. When people are excluded from many significant areas of society based on how God has fashioned them, this creates a deep emotional wound of trauma. Not just for the Black people that have the standards imposed upon them, but also for the White people that have to oppress Black people to feel superior and gain a competitive edge.

Who can critique God? The Bible teaches us that we are "fearfully and wonderfully made;" however, when people challenge the notion of what God has already ordained to be true, essentially, they are putting themselves in the position of gods. If God says that everything that I made is good and human beings are "very good ", then who are we to proclaim that only "some" people are good or "good enough"? This is a dangerous position to take as it idolizes man's opinion over God's.

Process Questions:

When you have looked at people of different ethnic backgrounds than yours have you ever discriminated based on their appearance?

Have you ever had the thought that they are not beautiful?

Have you excluded people from your group based on race, culture, or ethnicity?

Prayer for equity:
Father, help me to see the beauty in all of your creation. Reprogram the teachings of this world in my mind and heart. Help me to avoid putting standards upon people that you did not create.

When you look in the mirror, what standards of beauty do you find that you ascribe to?

How do these standards make you feel about yourself?

Day 21:
What About The Children?

1 Samuel 16:7

"But the Lord said to Samuel, "Do not look at his appearance or at the height of his stature, because I have rejected him. For the Lord sees not as man sees; for man looks [a]at the outward appearance, but the Lord looks at the heart."

Ruby Bridges was 6 years old when she became the first Black person to integrate a White school in the South. She faced cruel racial slurs and angry White mobs each day upon her entrance to her elementary school. She and her mother were reportedly escorted to the school each morning by four federal marshals. Hollywood has created films about the life of Ruby Bridges many times telling the story of a courageous young girl who overcame great odds. This story sounds very different than history depicts of racial terror inflicted upon a child. She revealed that the day she became frightened was when she saw a lady with a black doll in a coffin.

This young girl, while she may have been courageous, was still a girl. What child deserves this? Angry White adults hurled insults and threats at her and her mother. A disgusting display indeed. This was an attempt to maintain segregation and protest integration, many claiming that this is the way that God intended it to be. As an adult, Ruby Bridges released footage of the day that she went to school in a video entitled "The Children Were Watching". Angry White women and men were vehemently speaking about their hatred for Black people and their strong protest of desegregation as their children were standing by their side.

It would be easy to bypass the significance of the times as "a time past in history" and no longer relevant; however, Ruby Bridges was born on September 8, 1954, and is still living. While many people would like to believe that racism is over and we are far removed from it, nothing could be further from the truth. Those scars are very much alive and impacting people that are still walking this earth. Just as she is still alive, many of the people that took their place in history are alive as well. These people are said to be on the wrong side of history, displaying hate and malice for a 6-year-old child.

Process Questions:

What would motivate such a display of hatred?

What would cause mass numbers of people to protest desegregation?

Have you held malice, judgment, prejudice or discrimination in your heart?

People look upon others and decide what value they have, but God looks at the heart. God created everyone equally. People look at the outward appearance and determine how much value to assign, God sees and assess the heart motives.

How would you feel if you were in Ruby Bridges' position? Explain.

Prayer for humility:
Father, help me to avoid looking at the outward appearance of people and judging them. Give me a pure and Holy heart before you, void of hate.

Day 22:
Land of Opportunity

James 3:14

"14 But if you have bitter jealousy and selfish ambition in your hearts, do not be arrogant, and [as a result] be in defiance of the truth."

America is said to be the land of opportunity. Maybe for some, but this is and has not been the case for others. Affirmative Action was instituted as a means of leveling the playing field of opportunity in jobs, housing, education, etc. Affirmative Action is basically policies and practices implemented for the purpose of giving opportunities to historically underrepresented populations. Depending upon your history you may have a positive or negative view of Affirmative Action.

There have been many groups that have vehemently opposed Affirmative Action at its core, claiming that it is unconstitutional, "reverse racism", and a host of other things. However, no matter the view on Affirmative Action, it has been an attempt to desegregate society on all levels. You may have raised your eyebrows at this thought. Why would society still need to be desegregated you may ask?

Another question that is equally important is why would there be so many attempts to overturn legislation to resegregate society through abolishing Affirmative Action?

The quick answer to these questions is to keep power in the hands of the rich, powerful, and White. Opportunities can be passed down generationally as can wealth and knowledge. By keeping wealth and knowledge isolated to some and out of reach of others, society remains fixed, and structures of power are maintained. This is institutional racism operating at its finest. It does not matter what package it comes in; it is politicized sin. God hates prejudice and discrimination especially when it is motivated by pride, hate, and greed.

Process Questions:

When you hear the words Affirmative Action what images come to your mind?

What were you taught about it?

How do you feel about Affirmative Action as an idea?

What emotions come up for you?

Do you believe that Affirmative Action is necessary?

Prayer for equity:
Father, help me to avoid having bitter jealousy in my heart that seeks to keep others from opportunities. Help me to let go of selfish ambition and arrogance in my heart. Help me to accept the truth about my motives towards people that come from underrepresented groups. Give me opportunities to open doors for others that otherwise would remain shut.

What areas of influence do you currently have? How can you use your influence to provide opportunities for the underprivileged?

Day 23:
Inherently Inferior

James 3:15

"15 This [superficial] wisdom is not that which comes down from above, but is earthly (secular), natural (unspiritual), even demonic."

In 1619, prior to what we now call America, Africans were captured and enslaved. Slavery was justified by pseudoscientific ideas of racism to justify the inhumane and maltreatment of Black people as well as justify racial inequality. If the masses could be convinced that Black people are inherently inferior, then this would justify practices of White supremacy and hate of White people towards Black people.

Blacks were regulated to a less than human category. Article one, Section two of the United States Constitution is a present display of White Supremacy operating, delegating Black people to three-fifths of a person. How dehumanizing! Blacks were not considered full people, certainly much less than their White counterparts. Even more appalling, this heinous document built upon racist ideas and beliefs continues to govern our laws.

Craniometry was the measurement of skulls, which postulated that White people are biologically superior to Black people. This data was weaponized and became the catalyst for what we now know as racism in America. To be clear, race is a human construct birthed by these false notions and ideas.

Anti-Black hate and discrimination with origins in pseudoscience has long been disproven; however, they fuel many forms of systemic racism that carries the belief that Black people are predisposed to criminality. This type of rhetoric fuels Anti-Black hate crimes as well as over policing in Black neighborhoods, mass incarceration, and policies that target Black people with overly punitive laws and sentences.

While you may laugh at the preposterous notion that this could be considered real science, these so-called studies fuel White supremacy throughout society and even within many Christian circles. Post slavery, it was the gasoline to a growing problem of racial control, discrimination, and segregation that justified violence and extinction tactics of the Black race.

Process Questions:

Have you ever been taught about scientific racism?
What are your thoughts concerning scientific racism?
How do you think that your thoughts about Black
people have been impacted by this history?

What anti-Black stereotypes have you heard? List
them here.

Prayer for truth:
Father, help me to be a truth seeker
and turn my heart and mind away
from the lies of the enemy. I rebuke
the demonic forces attached to racism
operating in society today. Help me to
operate in your truth and wisdom and
reject secular knowledge.

List the ways that racial slurs & stereotypes shaped your thinking about people of different racial groups.

Day 24:
Justified Jealousy

James 3:16

"For where jealousy and selfish ambition exist, there is disorder [unrest, rebellion] and every evil thing and morally degrading practice."

On September 11, 2001, most people remember planes flying into the World Trade Center and the trauma and terror that resulted. However, this was not the first time that planes were used to terrorize Americans. In 1921 in Tulsa, Oklahoma bombs were dropped from the air on the city of Greenwood, killing approximately 300 Black Americans and injuring hundreds more.

The area destroyed was named Black Wall Street by Booker T. Washington. It was comprised of multiple Black millionaires and Black businesses. Unfortunately, this Black wealth and notoriety gained negative attention from the neighboring White community. Due to fake news, claiming that a Black man had assaulted a White girl in an elevator, White mobs of approximately 2000 people came together to avenge the alleged crime. Despite the fact that the White girl denied an assault and had not filed charges, the White mobs took things into their own hands. Among the White vigilantes, were also police officers serving their own hate-driven justice.

Tragically, no arrest or investigations were completed regarding this "ethnic cleansing" of sorts. How could this be? This day generational wealth was stolen, and thousands of Black people were left without homes. The Bible says that hatred is like murder. When we are consumed by hate, it is like a consuming fire. It destroys everything in its path. No good can come from a hate-filled heart. Hate has a way of clouding our judgment. It drives self-righteousness and vengeance. The heart of a hateful person is a playground for demonic activity.

Evil hides in the untold stories of painful histories. Sadly, many people have never heard of this travesty.

Process Questions:

How have you guarded your heart against the evils of racism, hate, and vengeance?

What is your response to this piece of buried history?

What emotions did you experience?

Consider day 24:

Write a reflection concerning the story shared.

What do you believe the residual impact of Black
Wall Street bombing is? Explain.

Day 25:
Assassinating Justice

Proverbs 21:15

"When justice is done, it is a joy to the righteous (the upright, the one in right standing with God), But to the evildoers it is disaster."

In August of 1968, the hit song "Say it Loud, I'm Black and I'm Proud" was released by James Brown. It was an anthem in the Black community that was not only fighting anti-Black racism, but also colorism among Black people. This song was a charge to the Black community to love the skin that they are in. This song was released four months after the assassination of Dr. Martin Luther King, Jr. His lyrics were paramount to everything that Dr. King fought for:

"Now we demand a chance to do things for ourselves
We're tired of beating our heads against the wall
And working for someone else, huh
You know, we are people, too
We like the birds and the bees
But we'd rather die on our feet
Than keep living on our knees
Say it loud (I'm Black and I'm proud)"

This is an important song, in a time when anti-Black hate was at a high. This was a significant song for America that sought to murder the Black race physically, psychologically, and economically. Every message that society screamed about Blackness was that it was something to be avoided, feared, and hated. During the time of Dr. King, there were two streams of consciousness regarding how the racial problem in America towards Blacks should be handled: through non-violence and "by any means necessary."

Dr. Martin Luther King, Jr. was inspired by the teachings of Jesus Christ and Gandhi, who also promoted non-violence. In a world where Black people had seen so much violence at the hands of White people, this seemed counterintuitive. Though many people celebrate Dr. King, many sought to put an end to him. There were multiple attempts on his life. He is quoted saying, ""The hottest place in Hell is reserved for those who remain neutral in times of great moral conflict." Dr. King called to the higher moral self, this transcended racial barriers into the human consciousness. He also said, "There comes a time when one must take a position that is neither safe, nor politic, nor popular, but he must take it because conscience tells him it is right."

The murder of Dr. King devastated not only the Black community, but also the Civil Rights Movement as it had lost a key leader. The Black community heavily grieved his death. How could someone that preached such heartfelt messages about the love of God, justice, non-violence, and brotherhood be brutally murdered? Dr. King was murdered, because he stood for Black people obtaining their God-given place in society. The right to be treated like a human. This was not a social cause, but rather a human right. An attempt to maintain White superiority and hatred were the poisons that ultimately murdered Dr. King.

1 John 3:15 says, "Everyone who hates (works against) his brother [in Christ] is [at heart] a murderer [by God's standards]; and you know that no murderer has eternal life abiding in him."

Process Questions:

How do you respond to this verse?

Are you guilty of murder?

What side of history would you have been on in Dr. King's Day?

What side of history are you currently on?

Prayer for Justice: Father, allow justice to be served so that every one of your children will know your joy. Preserve your Kingdom in each one of your children. Help us to stand upright before you, preserving what is right in your sight. Help us to put aside prejudice, racism, and hate.

Day 26:
Strange Fruit

If you are a classic jazz lover. You may have heard the 1939 song Strange Fruit performed by Billie Holiday. The lyrics give the visual of a lynching:

"Southern trees bear a strange fruit Blood on the leaves and blood at the root Black body swinging in the Southern breeze Strange fruit hanging from the poplar trees Pastoral scene of the gallant South The bulging eyes and the twisted mouth Scent of magnolia, sweet and fresh And the sudden smell of burning flesh! Here is a fruit for the crows to pluck For the rain to gather, for the wind to suck For the sun to rot, for a tree to drop, Here is a strange and bitter crop."

Racial terror against Black people in the United States is nothing new. There are over 4,000 documented lynchings, where people were beaten, hung, shot, burned and maimed and put on public display, recorded from 1877-1950. This was done to maintain White supremacy and Black fear and compliance. Many White people did not like the fact that Black people were formally viewed as property now were free and had equal rights. In many cases, the body parts of Black people were sold as souvenirs, pictures were taken with the hanging Black bodies, and images from the murder printed on postcards and stamps.

Lynchings in America have a dark history indeed. Racial terror lynchings were carnivalized, where refreshments and souvenirs were sold. Hundreds and thousands of White people would attend with their families to watch and partake in the murder of Black people. There has been little to no effort of legal prosecution for these acts of murder and violence towards Black people.

It may be difficult to process this information as it is detestable and demonic in nature. It is difficult to quote "love your neighbor" in this context as these acts far surpass what love is. In fact, these acts were more in alignment with Satan's agenda for people "to kill, steal, and destroy." Racism in America has an abominable history. Satan has used people to bring his evil plans to fruition. Sadly, many people who engaged in these events were confessed Christians and officers of the law.

Process Questions:

How could the moral compass be so off kilter?

What things have you been complacent with regarding the pain and racial terror that people of color have faced?

Consider Day 26: Share your thoughts and emotions concerning the text.

Write a prayer for people who are vulnerable to modern day lynching.

Prayer for justice:
Father, allow your judgment to come for those that commit evil acts of terror upon your children. Help me to not be complacent or an accomplice to these evil deeds. Open my eyes to the evils that are around me, let me see the truth.

Day 27:
Evil is in the DNA

Galatians 5:19

"19 When you follow the desires of your sinful nature, the results are very clear: sexual immorality, impurity, lustful pleasures,"

In 2006, the "Me Too" movement was publicized to expose sexual violation and harassment of founder Tarana Burke. Many celebrities also came forward with their stories of sexual abuse and violations. While many people have the support and media power to expose the transgression of sexual violence, people in the bondage of slavery in America were not afforded those same liberties.

Enslaved Black people were considered property by their White owners and by the government. The idea was a person can do whatever they want with their property, including sexually abuse, assault, and defile the bodies of Black women, men, and children. The Black enslaved body was viewed as a commodity to be used, sold, beaten, bred and brutalized at the will of the White slave master. Many people today cannot fathom the idea of not having rights over their own bodies. Imagine having your body subjected to the lustful desires of a stranger, oppressor, or anyone that was not your spouse. It is difficult to imagine, much less endure.

Many enslaved Blacks were raped repeatedly by White slave owners. Many times, rapes resulted in conceiving children who were also exploited by the cycle of abuse and trauma. According to the Department of Justice, the legal definition of rape is "The penetration, no matter how slight, of the vagina or anus with any body part or object, or oral penetration by a sex organ of another person, without the consent of the victim." How can a person that is enslaved and viewed as property give consent? Their bodies were not considered their own by White slave masters, the local law, or even the constitution. At this time, there was no one to report the crimes to. If an enslaved person did get the courage to report the crime to the spouse of the abuser, it would result in disbelief and further abuse.

Research demonstrates that trauma can be passed down through DNA. What happens when there is generational trauma and abuse? Racism and violence have been traumatic for not only Black people descending from slaves, but also the White people descending from Slave masters.

Process Questions:

What type of trauma has been passed down through the DNA of White people in America?

Is it possible that racism can also be passed down? What do you think?

What sinful desires do you think have been generationally passed to you through the DNA of your ancestors?

What observations do you make concerning your family DNA and generational curses have been passed down?

Prayer for healing:
Father, heal my bloodline from lustful and sinful desires and passions. Forgive me for engaging in lustful imaginations and immorality. Break every generational curse brought about as a result of slavery and racism that has been passed down through my DNA.

How do you believe God can use you to change your family DNA and break generational curses?

Day 28:
Terror-ism

Psalms 43:1

"Judge and vindicate me, O God; plead my case against an ungodly nation.

O rescue me from the deceitful and unjust man!"

Dr. Martin Luther King, Jr's famous quote still rings true today "And I must say tonight that a riot is the language of the unheard. And what is it America has failed to hear? It has failed to hear that the plight of the negro poor has worsened over the last twelve or fifteen years. It has failed to hear that the promises of freedom and justice have not been met." Some people that have a bit of historical understanding may disagree with this as Black people are no longer enslaved and being lynched from trees; however, racial terror has taken on a new form.

In May 2020 in Minneapolis, millions watched the video of the murder of George Floyd by police officer Derrick Chauvin with his knee on his neck while Floyd said, "I can't breathe." This phrase seemed to take on a life of its own with protests all over the world. People stood for justice for Floyd and many other unarmed Black men and women murdered by police officers. This seemed to be a collective cry for justice and freedom. These murders of Black people are not historically new; however, technology has made it possible to capture and share videos of these crimes all over the world. This is a modern-day lynching.

Black Lives Matter has been on the front lines of many protests demanding justice for these families. Opposing groups have also attended and infiltrated these protests. BLM has been labeled a terrorist group; however, there is no history of racial terror. This is in direct contrast to the Ku Klux Klan who has a long history of racial terror, murder, and racial violence against Blacks in America since 1865 when it was founded; however, the KKK has not been labeled a terrorist group. There have been petitions aiming to accomplish this.

What happens when the people cry out for justice and are met with violence? Many peaceful protests were met with police control through forceful means using tear gas to disperse crowds. This is in direct contrast to the January 6, 2021, riot at the Capitol building where police officers were threatened and the victims of violence. Less force was used in the latter case.

Process Questions:

Who does the oppressed cry out to when they are unheard?
Who should the oppressed contact when they are silenced?
What happens when the justice system is unjust?

- WHAT ARE YOUR THOUGHTS ABOUT DR. KING'S QUOTE?

- HOW DID YOU RESPOND TO THE MURDER OF GEORGE FLOYD?

- WHAT WAS YOUR REACTION TO THE RIOT AT THE CAPITAL?

- HOW DO YOU FEEL ABOUT BLM BEING CALLED A TERRORIST GROUP AND NOT THE KKK?

Choose two of the questions above and write a reflection.

Reflection 1

Reflection 2

Write your own version of the serenity prayer:

_____

_____

_____

_____

_____

_____

_____

_____

Prayer for justice:
Father, you see all things, just and unjust. Send your power and authority to rule over the unjust. Vindicate those that are suffering at the hands of the corrupt.

Day 29:
Shackled Truth

John 8:32 NLT

"32 And you will know the truth, and the truth will set you free."

The gospels of Jesus Christ have been long criticized by many religious skeptics as being contradictory to one another. This could not be further from the truth. These were eyewitness accounts. Just like any eyewitness account, you could expect a person to tell the story from their vantage point as well as when they entered the story. Their account makes it no less true, none-the-less, it is their account of what occurred.

In recent years, there has been much debate and conflict over Critical Race Theory (CRT), which is basically an academic and legal term that insists that racism in American society is a social construct and systemic. CRT takes the stance that racism is exponentially more than individual interactions of prejudice based on racial differences. It takes the stance that systems, laws, policies, and institutions reproduce racist policies that impact racist ideas and inequalities. This makes it possible to have racism without a racist people enacting acts of oppression. It becomes the system upholding these biases that ultimately keep Black, Indigenous, and people of color in a second-class status in society.

Many people have criticized CRT as they believe that when history is taught without white-washing it, it will impact the esteem and self-concept of White children. Others believe that for a proper education to be obtained, the fullness of history must be taught to all children because it is the truth. The sanitization of the horrors of American History have graced decades of academic books and lectures. This has also had the impact of erasure of other cultures that experienced history differently and many times more sinisterly.

This is particularly important when symbols of racism and people that inflicted violence upon marginalized groups are celebrated in history. These lessons have the capacity of becoming psychological trauma for marginalized groups in society and educational institutions.

An example of this is how changing the narrative of Thomas Jefferson being a founding father and author of the Declaration of Independence, but also owned and raped his slaves, tells a fuller story of who he was. Both are true; however, one side has been magnified as a truth in history books while the other side has been suppressed. CRT aims to expose both truths and validate historical narratives as they occurred absent of sanitization. When the truth is no longer silenced, it opens the doors for rectification and reconciliation.

Hosea 4:6 says, "My people are ruined because they don't know what's right or true.
Because you've turned your back on knowledge," Is it possible that we have rejected knowledge and truth?

Process Questions:

What has been the impact of suppressing truth?

Who has benefitted from this?

Who has been disadvantaged by suppression of truth?

What do you believe the impact of teaching the full truth of history to children will be?

Do you believe that teaching the sanitized version of American History promotes White Supremacy?

Prayer for truth:
Father, please reveal your truth to all people. Help us to open our eyes to truth, even if it is difficult to see. Allow your truth to set us free from the power of the sin of racism and ignorance.

Proverbs 17:15

"He who justifies the wicked, and he who condemns the righteous

Are both repulsive to the LORD."

A picture is said to speak a thousand words. The picture of 14-year-old Emmett Till lying in the casket disfigured was publicized following his brutal murder. His body was unrecognizable and could only be identified by the ring he wore on his finger. What could a child have done to warrant this type of cruelty? His mother Mamie Bradley made the decision to have her son's body photographed for the world to see the terror of racism and violence that her son endured.

Emmett Till was described as a fun-loving kid that was visiting his family in Mississippi from Chicago. He was accused of whistling at a White woman, Carolyn Bryant, in a store where he purchased candy. When her husband Roy Bryant returned home from a trip, he was informed of the alleged "disrespect" of his wife. He and his brother J.W. Milam went to Emmett Till's uncle's home, kidnapped him and savagely tortured and murdered him. They tortured, beat, shot, and tied a cotton gin engine to him and drowned him in the Tallahatchie River. His mutilated body surfaced three days later.

In the court case, the all-White jury deliberated for an hour and acquitted both men of the charges. They claimed that a positive ID could not be made due to disfigurement of his body. Both men later bragged about their heinous crimes against the child. Carolyn Bryant later recanted her story, denying that Emmett Till ever touched, threatened or harassed her. She reportedly said, "Nothing that boy did could ever justify what happened to him." This is tragic on many levels.

Process Questions:

What could ever justify this type of murderous rage?

What could justify complicity in the murder and acquittal of murderers?

How often have you watched injustice without intervening?

What emotions came up as you read this piece of history?

What thoughts came up as you read about what happened to Emmitt Till?

Prayer for justice: Father, bring justice to those that have been hurt by overt and covert racism. Help me to never justify the cruelty and wickedness of racism or passively witness the injustice of others.

Day 31:
Symbol-ism

1 Peter 2:1

"2 So put aside every trace of malice and all deceit and hypocrisy and envy and all slander and hateful speech"

Symbols can be an important and powerful marketing and communication tool. When we think of the slogan, "Just do it!" We immediately associate it with the swoosh, Nike symbol. When a symbol has been associated enough with its meaning, it can stand alone. At this point, the word "Nike" is no longer needed, and the message is still understood.

Throughout history symbols have been appropriated and used to instill fear and exact hate upon non-White groups. The Nazi swastika, which was stolen and altered from Indian religious traditions of the *Hakenkreuz* and used as a symbol of terror. Because symbols are powerful, many people no longer associate the symbol with prevailing, prosperity, and good. It has now been associated with the despicable mass genocide of Jews in the Holocaust. It has become a symbol of intolerance, hate, and superiority. The swastika symbol for many carries with it generational pain and mental scars of trauma.

John 10:10a is a powerful illustration of this. Satan is on a mission in the world to kill, steal, and destroy lives. Unfortunately, he has many misguided soldiers who have demonized racial and cultural differences and seek to exterminate those that are not like them in the name of good. Isaiah 5:20 says "Woe unto them that call evil good, and good evil; that put darkness for light, and light for darkness; that put bitter for sweet, and sweet for bitter!"

The Ku Klux Klan terrorist group identifies as a Christian group; however, they are known for burning crosses as a means of instilling fear. Why would a Christian group be responsible for burning the religion's most sacred symbol? They call them "cross lightings". They insist that this is done as a means of their faith in Christ. The question is then posed, why burn them on the lawns of Black people during racial terrorism? Deception is a powerful tool that inspires ignorance.

Process Questions:

How do you feel when you see a burning cross or a swastika?

What meaning do these symbols have for you?

How do you feel as a Christian seeing a cross set on fire?

What do you believe that this symbolizes?

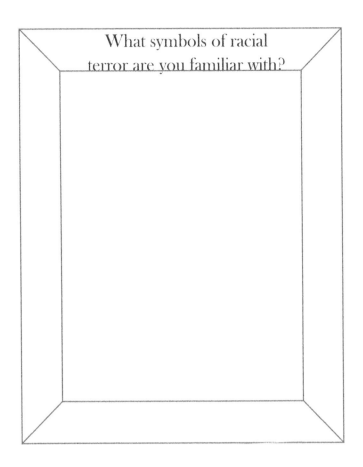

What symbols of racial
terror are you familiar with?

Prayer for repentance:
Father, help us to put away all symbols
of hate, malice, and intolerance. Help
us to avoid being deceived and falling
prey to the evils of racism in this world.
Forgive me for tolerating hate,
hypocrisy, and deceit.

Daily Faith Confessions & Commitment to Anti-racism

I rejoice in hope. I am patient in tribulation. I am constant in prayer *regarding racism*. (Romans 12:12)

I do not allow my heart to become hard towards racism. I understand with my heart the impact of racism. I allow God to heal me from the impact of racism. (John 12:40)

I accept God's grace to think soberly regarding myself. I have sound judgement. I have faith that things will get better *concerning racism*. (Romans 12:3)

I make no distinctions in God's people. (Galatians 3:28)

I respect the boundaries that have been established by God. (Acts 17:36)

I do not judge others by appearance. I am a fair judge (John 7:24)

God does not show favoritism. Neither will I. (Romans 2:11)

I fear God. I do what is right. (Acts: 10: 34-35)

I love myself. I love others also. (John 13:34)

I call on the Lord in faith and prayer *concerning racism*. (Romans 10:12)

I own my own sins and mistakes. I do not hold the sins of my ancestors. (Ezekiel 18:20)

I am made in the image of God. I uphold God's image in the earth. (Genesis 1:26-27)

I show no prejudice. (James 2:1)

I allow God's love for me to flow to how I love others. (1 Corinthians 13:1)

I do not have anything if I do not have love for others. (1 Corinthians 13:2)

I do what is right and judge with justice. (Leviticus 19:15)

Jesus died for me. God loves me. I trust Him. I am saved. I have eternal life. (John 3:16)

I respect others the way that I want to be respected. (Matthew 7:12)

I refuse to compare myself to others. (2 Corinthians 10:12)

I view people the way that God views them. (1 Samuel 16:7)

I am not in defiance of the truth. I am not arrogant, have selfish ambition or bitter jealousy in my heart. I refuse to be arrogant. (James 3:14)

I reject superficial wisdom that does not come from God. (James 3:15)

I reject jealousy, selfish ambition, unrest, and rebellion. I refuse to engage in evil and morally degrading practices. (James 3:16)

I act justly and righteously. I live uprightly and am in right standing with God. (Proverbs 21:15)

I am not confused. I do not call evil good and good evil. I do not substitute darkness for light and light for darkness. (Isaiah 5:20)

I refuse to follow the desires of this sinful nature. (Galatians 5:19)

I know the truth. I am free. (John 8:32)

I do not justify what is wicked. I do not condemn what is righteous. (Proverbs 17:15)

I refuse to display maliciousness, deceit, and hypocrisy. I will not envy or slander others with hateful speech. (1 Peter 2:1)

Congratulations! You made it this far.

Review your responses from Day 1 to Day 31. What commitments will you make to continue your journey of becoming an anti-racist? Be specific.

(Make a copy of this commitment to give to a trusted friend who will hold you accountable)

Made in the USA
Monee, IL
07 September 2023

42259977R00070